Dedicated to Grampa Pat

Grampa Pat was born in Chicago, Illinois and moved to Michigan in 1968 where he raised his family of four children, and later, happily spoiled four grandchildren. He is remembered fondly as being generous, caring and fun-loving. He enjoyed reading books to school children and visiting the elderly. His passion for reading, writing and learning led him to write a book of short stories and poems that promoted a strong moral compass. Grampa Pat is no longer with us, but his legacy lives on in his Furry Animal Tales. The Best Nut Party grew from his original idea, a creative spark we nourished and brought to life in these pages. We are honored to dedicate this book to him.

The Best Nut Party
Copyright © Vanessa Morley 2020

ISBN: 978-0-578-63105-9

THE Best NUT PARTY

words by Vanessa Morley

pictures by Camie Peasley

Sammy the squirrel was excited to find
all the nuts he had stored and left behind.

To celebrate his excitement and glee,
he thought of a way
he could hand them out for free.

Since walnuts and almonds are as precious as pearls,
he would plan a big nut party for all the squirrels.

This celebration was beginning to take form.
There'd be music and dancing, pecans and acorns.

Sammy knew the perfect spot to host his party,
where all the squirrels could be cheerful, loud and hearty.

There was a beautiful stream next to a large oak tree.
His friends would be happy with all they could see.

This oak tree happened to be Dr. Woo's place.
He could help you solve any problem you may face.

As Dr. Woo's name suggests he was a 'wise old owl.'
The animals went to him before they would growl.

Since there were so many nuts and preparations,
Sammy asked his siblings to help with decorations.

Ginger, his sister, and Rusty, his brother,
were always ready to support one another.

They began passing invitations out
to all the neighborhood squirrels who were out and about.

"Don't forget ANY squirrels!" Sammy advised.
He did not want anyone taken by surprise.

The day of the nut party was finally here.
It would be the best party in the forest this year.

Ginger and her friend Misty were a bit tardy
and happened to be the only girls at the party.

Sammy heard rumbling and grumbling as they sat down.
"What's all the fuss?" he asked with a frown.

"Is there something wrong with the nuts?" he pondered aloud.
Then suddenly a voice came from out of the crowd.

"Look at her fur! I've never seen such a sight.
Imagine a gray squirrel. Why, it just isn't right!"

Another one shouted, "A girl was invited?
Girls are not welcome! The boys stand united."

"What's wrong with girls?" Ginger started to yell.
This was not a good party, Sammy could tell.

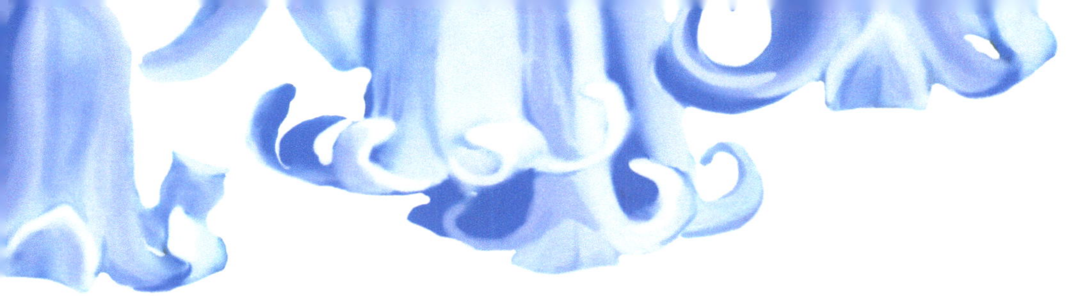

Sammy had to do something, without question.
Time was running short; he needed a suggestion.

So he looked up to see if Dr. Woo's office was busy,
and scurried up the tree so fast he was dizzy.

Line
starts
here

He didn't even look at the sign.
He just ran right past all the animals in line.

Dr. Woo was surprised and asked Sammy,
    "What's the matter?"
Sammy had to catch his breath before he started to chatter.

He told Dr. Woo about the way Misty was treated,
and how all the squirrels' tempers were way overheated.

Dr. Woo paused and thought for a while,
then spoke with assertion yet keeping his smile.

"Sammy sometimes you just need to stand up and do good,
to make a stand for the those who are misunderstood."

"Tell the squirrels to stop acting so nutty, so mad!
To disapprove of a fellow squirrel,
why, that would make them feel sad."

"The color of fur is not important
    like they think,
even if your fur is blue,
    red, green, or pink."

"They're all squirrels alike on this wonderful earth
and girls, just like boys, have the exact same worth."

"Now go tell them what I've said
        and make your voice be heard.
Time to make right this injustice that occurred."

So Sammy thanked Dr. Woo for all of his aid
and rushed back to the party bold and unafraid.

He came right up to the chattering crowd
and yelled, "QUIET EVERYONE!" so confident and loud.

ONE!

He repeated the wise words Dr. Woo gave
and one by one the squirrels began to behave.

They knew in their hearts they had acted all wrong,
and said sorry for making Misty feel like she didn't belong.

Misty forgave them
        and felt touched in her heart.
Then she said, "Time to begin this
        nut party with a fresh start."

And so this became known as the
        best nut party throughout the woods.
Forest animals from all around
        were inspired to do good.

Look around you, like Sammy,
        and find courage to stand tall.
In the face of meanness,
        you surely will not fall.

There is kindness in your heart, love and light.
Let it shine from within you,
it will make the world glow bright!

Vanessa Morley

Vanessa Morley is an entrepreneur, author, wife and mother of four beautiful children. She was born in Ontario, Canada and moved to Michigan after marrying her husband, Levi.

Transforming one of Grampa Pat's original stories into a rhyming picture book has been a fun way of creating meaningful family memories with her children in honor of their great-grampa Pat. Vanessa hopes this story inspires readers to be kind and forgiving toward others.

Camie Peasley

Camie Peasley is a digital painter, whose current art studio is inside her computer. The illustrations in this book were first sketched on paper and painted by hand using a pen tablet. Each image has over one hundred layers of colorful brushstrokes mixed with photographic textures. Camie enjoys making vibrant images that young readers can visually explore.

Many details in this book are native to Michigan where she lives with her husband, daughter and two sons. Camie works full time teaching children visual arts, and, like the squirrels in this book, encourages her students to always choose kindness.